Commentaries on Buddhahood

"On Attaining Buddhahood in This Lifetime"

THE SOKA GAKKAI STUDY DEPARTMENT

World Tribune
Press

Published by

World Tribune Press

606 Wilshire Blvd.

Santa Monica, CA 90401

Design by Gopa & Ted2, Inc.

13-digit ISBN 978-1-932911-20-6

10-digit ISBN 1-932911-20-0

10 9 8 7 6 5 4 3 2 1

Contents

Editor's Note

THIS LECTURE was originally given by SGI Study Department Leader Katsuji Saito for the SGI North America Leaders Study Conference held from July 15-17, 2005.

Please see *The Writings of Nichiren Daishonin*, pp. 3–5, for the full text of "On Attaining Buddhahood in This Lifetime."

The following abbreviations appear in some citations:

+ OTT, page number(s)—refers to *The Record of the Orally Transmitted Teachings*, translated by Burton Watson (Soka Gakkai: Tokyo, 2004)

+ WND, page number(s)—refers to *The Writings of Nichiren Daishonin* (Soka Gakkai: Tokyo, 1999)

"On Attaining Buddhahood in This Lifetime"

Background

IT IS ASSUMED that Nichiren Daishonin was thirty-four when he wrote this letter to Toki Jonin in 1255. Nichiren established his teaching in 1253, at thirty-two. This letter was written two years after that, around the time he began propagating his teaching in Kamakura, the seat of the shogunate government. In the letter, he explains the meaning of Nam-myoho-renge-kyo, which he had started to spread.

Many believers had by now taken faith in Nichiren's teaching, including Shijo Kingo, the Ikegami brothers, Kudo Yoshitaka and others. Toki Jonin is thought to have taken faith around 1254.

He had been serving Lord Chiba, the constable of Shimosa Province, likely as a steward or secretary to the Chiba family. Toki Jonin was well educated, and he received many important writings from Nichiren, including "The Object of Devotion for Observing the Mind," "On Taking the Essence of the Lotus Sutra" and "On the Four Stages of Faith and the Five Stages of Practice."

Key Points

In this letter, Nichiren Daishonin explains that chanting Nam-myoho-renge-kyo equals perceiving the "mystic truth" inherent in one's life. By chanting, people can tap their innate Buddha potential and purify their lives, thus attaining Buddhahood in this lifetime.

He admonishes us, however, that if we seek the Law outside ourselves, then we cannot attain Buddhahood no matter how much we chant Nam-myoho-renge-kyo.

He also teaches that we should regard chanting Nam-myoho-renge-kyo as the source of our benefit and that by so doing we polish our lives.

Nichiren concludes by explaining the profound meaning of Myoho-renge-kyo as the Law innate in life, and he urges Toki Jonin: "Maintain your faith and attain Buddhahood in this lifetime. Nam-myoho-renge-kyo, Nam-myoho-renge-kyo" (WND, 4). He clarifies that what is most important in Nichiren Buddhism is to develop faith in order to manifest the condition of Buddhahood in this lifetime.

Buddhism expounds upon the Law innate in life so that people can correctly navigate life's challenges. By believing in Nam-myoho-renge-kyo as the Law existing within us and continuing to chant it, we can polish our lives and definitely solidify our Buddhahood in this lifetime. This is the main point of this letter.

From the very beginning, Nam-myoho-renge-kyo has been the central teaching of Nichiren Buddhism. Nichiren chanted Nam-myoho-renge-kyo throughout his life. He also entrusted his disciples with spreading this great Law throughout Japan and the rest of the world as an antidote to the suffering of people of the Latter Day of the Law. Upon awakening to the ultimate teaching of Buddhism, Nichiren propagated it by expounding its essence—the Law of Nam-myoho-renge-kyo.

In "On Attaining Buddhahood in This Lifetime," two years after having declared his teaching, Nichiren clarified the meaning of Nam-myoho-renge-kyo. So it is most important for us to deepen our confidence in Nichiren Buddhism through studying this letter and to share the power of chanting Nam-myoho-renge-kyo with those who are unaware of it.

Additionally, by studying this letter, we will understand that it is only the SGI that has been practicing and propagating this great Law of Nam-myoho-renge-kyo exactly as intended by Nichiren.

Overcoming the
Sufferings of Birth and Death

If you wish to free yourself from the sufferings of birth and death you have endured since time without beginning and to attain without fail unsurpassed enlightenment in this lifetime, you must perceive the mystic truth that is originally inherent in all living beings. This truth is Myoho-renge-kyo. Chanting Myoho-renge-kyo will therefore enable you to grasp the mystic truth innate in all life. (WND, 3)

TO FREE OURSELVES from the sufferings of birth and death, we must perceive the mystic truth inherent in all living beings. To do this, Nichiren Daishonin writes, we must chant Myoho-renge-kyo.

"Birth and death you have endured since time without beginning" refers to the eternal cycle of death and rebirth. Without understanding the meaning of birth and death, this endless repetition becomes eternally unbearable suffering. For this reason, in the Buddhist tradition, the phrase *birth and death* is an expression of suffering.

When people are suffering a great deal, it is unbearable for them to think of repeating the experience in successive lifetimes for all eternity. It is understandable then that they may wish to exit the cycle of death and rebirth and somehow enjoy peace and security outside it.

Nichiren writes that we will "attain without fail unsurpassed enlightenment in this lifetime." Here, he places particular emphasis on the present lifetime out of the countless lifetimes one has lived thus far. "Unsurpassed enlightenment" means awakening to the truth by which we can transcend the sufferings of life and death.

It is our good fortune to have been born as human beings, because we have the capacity to stop experiencing the process of birth and death as an endless cycle of suffering and to attain the same enlightenment as the Buddha. To seize this great opportunity—in this lifetime—we must perceive the "mystic truth that is originally inherent in all living beings."

The Mystic Truth Within All Living Beings

This mystic truth is the essential Law of the universe that supports all things. A Buddha is someone who has attained enlightenment through realizing that at the root of his or her life exists this Law.

This truth is difficult to perceive clearly or understand intellectually. It is therefore called "mystic." The mystic truth is the unfathomable Law.

The Mystic Law is the fundamental principle that supports the universe and gives rise to all phenomena. The word *Law* in Buddhism is a translation of the Sanskrit word *dharma*, one meaning of which is "to sustain" or "to support."

We can understand the support function of a law by looking at the laws of society. For instance, we have laws that support the traffic system and laws that support commercial transactions. Such laws, then, function to support the orderly conduct of society.

In addition to laws established by humans, there are many others that govern different aspects of life and nature, such as the laws of physics and biology.

What gives rise to all those laws is the Mystic Law. It is the essential Law that supports all things. Because it is difficult to comprehend, it is called "mystic" or "wonderous."

At the center of Nam-myoho-renge-kyo is *myoho*—which translates as the Mystic Law.

Because the Mystic Law underlies all things, naturally it supports all living beings. In other words, the Mystic Law exists in and supports our own lives. This is why Nichiren calls it the "mystic truth that is originally inherent in all living beings." But, he explains, unless we perceive this mystic truth, we cannot attain the supreme enlightenment of the Buddha or stop the endless suffering of birth and death.

People must perceive the Mystic Law, which is difficult to do. Many are likely to think: *We ordinary people cannot accomplish this. A Buddha is an extremely special individual who can perform such a difficult task.*

In this passage, however, Nichiren says something extraordinary: In this lifetime, *anyone* can perceive within his or her ordinary life this inherent mystic truth and thus become freed from the sufferings of birth and death. This is an amazing statement.

Everyone, explains Nichiren, can have in this lifetime what

in most religions would likely be reserved only for an elite group. From this first passage, he is declaring a religious teaching of profound greatness.

The Meaning of Myoho-renge-kyo

Even more amazing, Nichiren identifies this mystic truth inherent in all living beings as Myoho-renge-kyo, the name of the essential Law. When one chants the name of this Law, he says, it is the same as perceiving this mystic truth.

Shakyamuni realized the Mystic Law through his wisdom and tried to teach his disciples the practice to gain the same wisdom for themselves. Nichiren, however, teaches us to chant Nam-myoho-renge-kyo with confidence that the Mystic Law exists within. Chanting Nam-myoho-renge-kyo is an expression of that confidence, the proof of our faith. It demonstrates our intent to live in accordance with the Law. At the same time, it is an affirmation that our existence is essentially based on this Law.

Nichiren says, "Chanting Myoho-renge-kyo will therefore enable you to grasp the mystic truth innate in all life." In other words, chanting Myoho-renge-kyo equals perceiving the mystic truth. By chanting, we can live in the same way as those who perceive this truth. The greatness of Nichiren Buddhism lies in the discovery of this path to the ultimate reality.

Before the appearance of Nichiren, the Mystic Law was hinted at through metaphor but never directly explained. To arouse people's seeking spirit, teachers prior to Nichiren would emphasize the greatness of the Buddha awakened to this Law.

Unlike in those previous efforts, Nichiren opened the way for all people to manifest this mystic truth—by developing confidence in the existence of the Law within and by chanting its name.

When this mystic truth is activated in human life, it becomes the life of Buddhahood. The unlimited power of the Mystic Law is unleashed, hindered by nothing, and manifests as a human being's various strengths.

For example, the Mystic Law is revealed in human life as courage, perseverance, wisdom with which to break through obstacles, and compassion for others. These various powers—described as the attributes of the Buddha's life—immediately come forth from within. By chanting Nam-myoho-renge-kyo with confidence in its existence, this mystic truth and, with it, the condition of Buddhahood, will appear.

It should be noted that what prevents the power of the Mystic Law from manifesting is what Buddhism terms *the fundamental darkness*—our own, deep-rooted delusion or ignorance.

Fundamental darkness is a foundational ignorance of the Mystic Law that leads us into a state of confusion. It causes us to fall under the influence of dark impulses that steer us to unhappiness. In other words, fundamental darkness is the root of all suffering and unhappiness.

Once we awaken to the Mystic Law, then, this fundamental darkness will be dispelled. To illustrate, if we compare the Mystic Law to the sun, then fundamental darkness may be likened to clouds covering it. When the dark clouds are dissipated, bright rays of sunlight immediately shoot through. When we dispel our fundamental ignorance, the power of the Mystic Law begins to work at once, creating benefit and value in our lives. The benefits and positive values that appear in our lives as we affirm the Mystic Law inherent within us can be likened to the lotus blossom, or *renge*, which blooms out of a muddy swamp. In this way, Myoho-renge-kyo is the life of a Buddha that is at one with the Law.

Although all people are entities of the Mystic Law and originally endowed with the life of Buddhahood, unless they fight off the dark clouds of fundamental darkness, their Buddhahood will not actually emerge. Simply chanting Nam-myoho-renge-kyo as if it were a magic incantation will not enable us to manifest our innate Buddhahood.

As mentioned, Myoho-renge-kyo is the essential Law of the universe, and the greatness of Nichiren Buddhism lies in its essential practice: chanting the name of the Law. To firmly establish this path to revealing our Buddhahood, however, we must wage an inner battle against the fundamental darkness in our hearts. To describe this struggle in a word, it is *faith*.

Based on his penetrating examination of the Lotus Sutra, which reveals the Buddha's enlightenment, Nichiren discovered Myoho-renge-kyo—the life of a Buddha—within his own life. Through his own struggle, he proved the existence of the Mystic Law within. For us to bring forth that Myoho-renge-kyo, we must chant Nam-myoho-renge-kyo in the same manner as Nichiren. Underlying our chanting must be the spirit to fight off the fundamental darkness—this is the true spirit of faith. We might say, then, that the *daimoku*, or Nam-myoho-renge-kyo, Nichiren spread was a "fighting daimoku."

Fundamental darkness appears in various forms, such as

doubt, insecurity, suffering and so on. One can only defeat all these through the power of faith. This is why Nichiren often emphasizes doubt-free faith. Also, as he states, "The single word 'belief' is the sharp sword with which one confronts and overcomes fundamental darkness or ignorance" (*The Record of the Orally Transmitted Teachings*, pp. 119–20).

What we need most is the "sharp sword" of faith or conviction. Challenging life's negative functions essentially means battling the fundamental darkness. Currently, we are challenging the influence of the Nichiren Shoshu priesthood, which is trying to obstruct kosen-rufu. At the deepest level, the struggle against the priesthood's negative function is the same as our struggle against the fundamental darkness. (For more information on the Nichiren Shoshu priesthood, visit sokaspirit.org)

Whenever we confront life's various obstacles, we are essentially challenging our fundamental darkness. If we lose our faith —our conviction in the potential for absolute happiness, for ourselves and others, we will succumb to those obstacles.

Chanting entails two aspects: faith and practice. Faith, or confidence, is the crucial element of an effective attitude when chanting Nam-myoho-renge-kyo. Practice has two components. As an affirmation of our developing faith, we chant Nam-myoho-renge-kyo to the Gohonzon. This is the aspect of practice for ourselves. As we continue, we will naturally develop our compassion toward others, which gives rise to the urge to share with them this way to tap the wonderful life of Myoho-renge-kyo. Giving expression to that desire is the aspect of practice for others.

The core of chanting Nam-myoho-renge-kyo is the

development of our conviction, our confidence. Only through our spiritual struggle to develop confidence—to apply both the faith and practice aspects of chanting Nam-myoho-renge-kyo, and to practice for both self and others—can we "grasp the mystic truth innate in all life." This is the only recipe for bringing forth the power of Buddhahood.

The Mutually Inclusive Relationship of Life at Each Moment and All Phenomena

Nichiren Daishonin equates "the mystic truth innate in all life" with "the mutually inclusive relationship of life at each moment and all phenomena." By doing so, he emphasizes the importance of the mind.

It is called the Mystic Law because it reveals the principle of the mutually inclusive relationship of a single moment of life and all phenomena. That is why this sutra is the wisdom of all Buddhas. Life at each moment encompasses the body and mind and the self and environment of all sentient beings in the Ten Worlds as well as all insentient beings in the three thousand realms, including plants, sky, earth, and even the minutest particles of dust. Life at each moment permeates the entire realm of phenomena and is revealed in all phenomena. To be awakened to this principle is itself the mutually inclusive relationship of life at each moment and all phenomena. (WND, 3)

"Life at each moment" and "a single moment of life" refer to a person's mind at this present instant, also known as a "life-moment." "All phenomena" refers to the universe itself as well as everything in it.

From the Buddhist viewpoint, one's life at each moment contains everything in the universe, including the minutest particle of dust. At the same time, one's life at each moment permeates the entire universe. This truth is revealed in the teaching of the "mutually inclusive relationship of life at each moment and all phenomena." This is also referred to as the "three thousand realms in a single moment of life."

One's life—which is the entity of the Mystic Law—embraces his or her whole environment, the entire universe. This is the basis of the principle that if we change, our world changes as well. It is also related to the doctrines of human revolution and that by establishing the correct teaching we can obtain the peace of the land.

What really matters is ourselves. Whatever happens, no one else is to blame. Everything we undergo is for our own sake. Unless we deeply understand this, we cannot fully perceive the Mystic Law within our lives.

SGI President Ikeda writes: "A great human revolution in just a single individual will help achieve a change in the destiny of a nation and, further, will enable a change in the destiny of all humankind'—this was the conviction that dominated all my writing" (*The Human Revolution*, vol. 1, p. viii).

"The concept of human revolution might be thought of as a modern formulation of the Buddhist principle of a single life-moment encompassing three thousand realms. A transformation in the inner reality of our lives, in our minds, produces changes in the workings of our own lives (the realm of the five components), in other people (the realm of living beings) and also in the land (the realm of the environment).

"A change in our determination first produces a change in the inner reaches of our lives; it enables us to manifest qualities of excellent health, abundant strength and boundless wisdom. Lives that have been transformed in this way will lead others in the direction of happiness and will be committed to vanquishing evil. They will also have an impact on society and on the natural environment, transforming both into a paradise of peace and prosperity" (September 5, 1994, *World Tribune*, p. 3).

My Life Is an Entity
of the Mystic Law

Nevertheless, even though you chant and believe in Myoho-renge-kyo, if you think the Law is outside yourself, you are embracing not the Mystic Law but an inferior teaching. "Inferior teaching" means those other than this [Lotus] sutra, which are all expedient and provisional. No expedient or provisional teaching leads directly to enlightenment, and without the direct path to enlightenment you cannot attain Buddhahood, even if you practice lifetime after lifetime for countless kalpas. Attaining Buddhahood in this lifetime is then impossible. Therefore, when you chant *myoho* and recite *renge,*[1] you must summon up deep faith that Myoho-renge-kyo is your life itself. (WND, 3)

NICHIREN DAISHONIN admonishes us that although we chant Nam-myoho-renge-kyo, if we think that it exists outside ourselves, then what we practice is no longer the Mystic Law. It would be an inferior teaching. Therefore, we could not attain Buddhahood in this lifetime.

For this reason, he teaches, each of us must develop the conviction that "my life at each moment is Myoho-renge-kyo," that "Myoho-renge-kyo is my life itself" and that "the name of my life is Myoho-renge-kyo." We must chant Nam-myoho-renge-kyo with this sort of confidence, he says, which will enable us to attain Buddhahood in this lifetime.

Nichiren says, "If you think the Law is outside yourself...." Here, he refers to viewing Buddhism as a teaching concerned with externals rather than being about oneself. For example, some may revere Buddhas and bodhisattvas but view their own lives as insignificant or even dishonorable. This means they are looking at Buddhas and bodhisattvas as a special class of human beings, the very act of which disparages themselves. For this reason, even if such people appear to have strong faith, they actually conceive of their lives as having nothing to do with Myoho-renge-kyo.

The Pure Land school exemplifies this way of thinking. The Pure Land school teaches that Amida Buddha lives in the Pure Land of Perfect Bliss far to the west and that he will take the faithful to this Pure Land in the afterlife. Pure Land Buddhism teaches that the Buddha exists neither within one's life nor in this world and that Buddhas and bodhisattvas have no direct relationship with those living in the here and now.

Any religion that seeks salvation in the abstract or the absolute tends to focus on things far removed from ordinary people.

Furthermore, such religions tend to give rise to intermediaries between the absolute (e.g., God, the Buddha) and ordinary people. By virtue of being closer to the Buddha or God, the clergy is viewed as superior to ordinary people. That sort of discriminatory view, which is the essence of the Nichiren Shoshu priesthood, is also a way of thinking that "the Law is outside yourself."

Nichiren clarifies that to chant Nam-myoho-renge-kyo with this perspective is not the correct practice to enable one to attain Buddhahood in this lifetime. This letter, written early in Nichiren's undertaking of his mission for widespread human happiness, is already a refutation of the Nichiren Shoshu priesthood.

Since the inception of the Soka Gakkai under the first president, Tsunesaburo Makiguchi, members have regarded Buddhism as a teaching about their own lives, about their attainment of Buddhahood and about establishing peace in their world. Based on this Buddhist view, SGI members have been developing their faith and chanting Nam-myoho-renge-kyo, which is why kosen-rufu has made such great progress.

Members of the Nichiren Shoshu priesthood, concerned only with priestly privilege, reacted negatively to the SGI's view of faith. While some priests recognized the correctness of the SGI, the majority tended to abuse their religious authority.

During Japan's feudal age, there was a government-sponsored parish system that encouraged Buddhist priests to exert great authority over ordinary people. This system promoted for the lay believers a subservient relationship to the priests. The Nichiren Shoshu priesthood strongly asserts such priestly authority today. Nikken Abe, the previous high priest, attempted to destroy the religion dedicated to kosen-rufu built by the Soka Gakkai in favor of reviving a priest-centered doctrine. Because of the high priest's actions in this regard, we say that the Nichiren Shoshu priesthood committed slander of the Law. The priesthood has strayed fundamentally from Nichiren Buddhism. As Nichiren says, "If you think the Law is outside yourself, you are embracing not the Mystic Law but an inferior teaching."

Here, "an inferior teaching" refers to teachings that are incomplete or disingenuous. We can consider this passage as Nichiren's refutation of the Nichiren Shoshu priesthood.

In general, religion tends to center on the clergy. But Nichiren was opposed to this. Based on the Lotus Sutra's essential ideal that all people can attain Buddhahood, Nichiren transcended religion's clergy-centered tendency and its potential for authoritarianism. From the beginning, his Buddhism has been a teaching of reform—he established his central teaching of chanting Nam-myoho-renge-kyo as the way for all people to attain Buddhahood.

In this letter, Nichiren expounds on the meaning of chanting Nam-myoho-renge-kyo, the foundation and practice of Nichiren Buddhism. Because he repeatedly admonishes us not to seek the Law outside ourselves, we can transcend the destiny of other religions that fall into formality and authoritarianism.

Nichiren's admonition not to seek the Law outside ourselves may be considered his fundamental standard for evaluating religion. If we view the Law as outside us rather than as innate within all human beings, we become prone to disparaging others (or ourselves) and to undervaluing the importance of fighting for each person's happiness. Religions that promulgate an external source of salvation tend to devolve into schools in which maintaining the authority and livelihood of the clergy at all costs becomes the basis of religious practice. Nichiren's admonition in this letter is a general refutation of this tendency.

In our practice, we strive to chant with the confidence that Myoho-renge-kyo is our lives. We challenge ourselves to chant Nam-myoho-renge-kyo with firm conviction in our capacity for absolute happiness and for manifesting Buddhahood in this lifetime. Furthermore, we strive to practice for the happiness of others. This has been the orientation of Soka Gakkai members since the beginning.

About this passage, President Ikeda comments: "He is urging us to decide and believe that we ourselves are entities of *Myoho-renge-kyo*. The Mystic Law is the great beneficial medicine for relieving the sufferings of all people. It is also the wonderful treasure trove for realizing human happiness. We need to live out our lives based on and dedicated to the Mystic Law. We need to fill and solidify our lives with this great Law" (*The World of Nichiren Daishonin's Writings*, vol. 1, p. 127).

"I am Myoho-renge-kyo"—each of us must so decide. It is up to you. It is you who makes your life one with the Mystic Law. This is what was in Nichiren's heart when he taught Myoho-renge-kyo. With this Law of Myoho-renge-kyo, we become genuinely happy and help many others do the same. We bring peace to our nations and to the whole world. This is Nichiren Buddhism. The basis of all these is Myoho-renge-kyo.

President Ikeda continues: "The Mystic Law is eternal. It is the wellspring of all things. When we perceive that our life is one with the Mystic Law, we experience the eternity of life and boundless energy wells forth. Nothing can destroy this. No matter what happens, we enjoy a state of complete freedom. That is the life-state of Buddhahood. Therein lies the profound significance of chanting Myoho-renge-kyo" (ibid, vol. 1, pp. 127–28).

Myoho-renge-kyo is the fundamental, eternal Law of the universe. All phenomena appear from the depths of the great ocean called the Mystic Law and return to it. All things are in a constant state of flux. What is eternal is only the Mystic Law, which gives rise to and embraces all things. The state of Buddhahood enables us to freely manifest the unlimited power of the Mystic Law in our lives and in our actions. Our lives are inherently at one with the Mystic Law. To help all people experience the benefit of being at one with the Mystic Law is the purpose of the teaching of Myoho-renge-kyo.

Renge, the lotus blossom, indicates the Mystic Law's unlimited power to create positive value. Through this power, many benefits blossom from within our lives. As the teaching of "the true aspect of all phenomena" explains, all things are manifestations of the Mystic Law.

As mentioned earlier, however, when the dark clouds of disbelief and delusion envelope our lives, we cannot reveal the unlimited power of the Mystic Law. This is the cause for the sufferings of birth and death in lifetime after lifetime. We can stop this by breaking through delusion and ignorance with faith, thereby revealing ours lives as the complete manifestations of Myoho-renge-kyo.

Those who have done so are Buddhas, and to do so is the purpose of our lives. We have been born as human beings in order to savor the power of the Law of Myoho-renge-kyo.

Humans have the superior mental capacity to make this possible, but because of the workings of our minds, we humans also experience a great deal of suffering. Some may even think that the sole purpose of the human mind is to create suffering. But when we come to realize that the meaning of our lives is to completely enjoy the power of Myoho-renge-kyo, we can then view hardships as the spice of life with which we can savor the Law's wonderful taste.

In this regard, Josei Toda, the second Soka Gakkai president, states: "Attaining enlightenment does not mean becoming a Buddha or trying to become a Buddha. Rather, it means awakening to the fact that we were and will be a Buddha from the eternal past into the eternal future. This is in accordance with our sincere belief in Nichiren's teaching that ordinary people can manifest the supremely noble state of Buddhahood, just as they are, and the concept of the 'true aspect of all phenomena'... The fact that we are ordinary people is a secret and mystic expedient, and the truth is that we are Buddhas. The Gohonzon also exists within us. In other words, deep faith means to believe that the Gohonzon inside our altars is our lives" (*Toda Josei zenshu* [Collected Writings of Josei Toda] vol. 3).

Sincere and honest faith—this is what is most important. To develop such conviction, however, is a most difficult task, for we often allow the "lesser ego" to control our lives.

The reality of life is that it is a succession of worries, one after another. For this reason, it is important to decide: *My life is Myoho-renge-kyo*. With this realization, we can courageously challenge and triumph over all manner of worries. With confidence that we are Myoho-renge-kyo, we never have to run away; we can challenge every obstacle head on. Whether we can bring forth courage as an expression of our confidence, or faith, is the key to victory in life.

Overcoming our cowardice and bringing forth the courage to challenge each obstacle—this is what is most important. No matter what negativity arises, we must challenge it all without retreating even a step; we must develop profound confidence that we have enough power to do this. That power is Myoho-renge-kyo.

On the contrary, if you fear and complain about your obstacles, you are choosing to believe that "the Law is outside yourself." Each of us must guard against this pitfall.

Nichiren writes, "Nichiren's disciples cannot accomplish anything if they are cowardly" ("The Teaching, Practice, and Proof," WND, 481). He also proclaims the need to have the "courage of a lion king" ("On Persecutions Befalling the Sage," WND, 997).

What is most important is to develop courage based on faith. When the dark clouds are dispelled, the sun, which was always there, illuminates the whole world. Likewise, when we challenge all obstacles by bringing forth our courage, our inherent Buddhahood emerges. Nam-myoho-renge-kyo is the life of Buddhahood that arises through courageous faith. Faith, or conviction, is the cause and Buddhahood is its effect—and cause and effect are one. This entire causality of Buddhahood is called Nam-myoho-renge-kyo.

Nichiren writes, "You must summon up deep faith that Myoho-renge-kyo is your life itself" (WND, 3). Unless we chant Nam-myoho-renge-kyo with such faith, or courage, we are not practicing the Myoho-renge-kyo that Nichiren taught and propagated.

NOTE:

1. "Chant *myoho* and recite *renge*" means to chant the daimoku of the Mystic Law, or Nam-myoho-renge-kyo.

The Nature of One's Life

You must never think that any of the eighty thousand sacred teachings of Shakyamuni Buddha's lifetime or any of the Buddhas and bodhisattvas of the ten directions and three existences are outside yourself. Your practice of the Buddhist teachings will not relieve you of the sufferings of birth and death in the least unless you perceive the true nature of your life. If you seek enlightenment outside yourself, then your performing even ten thousand practices and ten thousand good deeds will be in vain. It is like the case of a poor man who spends night and day counting his neighbor's wealth but gains not even half a coin. That is why the T'ien-t'ai school's commentary states, "Unless one perceives the nature of one's life, one cannot eradicate one's grave offenses."[1] This passage implies that, unless one perceives the nature of one's life, one's practice will become an endless, painful austerity. Therefore, such students of Buddhism are condemned as non-Buddhist. *Great Concentration and Insight* states that, although they study Buddhism, their views are no different from those of non-Buddhists. (WND, 3–4)

NICHIREN DAISHONIN again admonishes us not to seek Buddhist teachings outside our lives. If we do, then, although we perform "even ten thousand practices and ten thousand good deeds," we cannot free ourselves from suffering. It is as futile as counting our neighbor's wealth. Ultimately, all of our efforts will be wasted. For this reason, Nichiren urges us to "perceive the true nature of our lives" by seeking the ultimate Law of Myoho-renge-kyo within us.

If we seek the Law outside us, we will not find it no matter how hard we try, and therefore our efforts will be an "endless, painful austerity. Our karma will remain the same, without the slightest change, and everything will become the cause of further suffering.

By maintaining the attitude that Buddhism is applicable only to others or to externals, we limit or trivialize our own lives. As mentioned earlier, some think that there are wonderful Buddhas and bodhisattvas who exist apart from where they themselves are. Others believe they will be reborn into another world or paradise. These perspectives correspond to thinking the Law is outside oneself.

The Lotus Sutra, however, teaches that the Mystic Law is revealed in our lives. Buddhas and Buddha lands exist nowhere but within us, not in some far-away place. Nichiren Buddhism —more specifically, the practice of chanting Nam-myoho-renge-kyo—helps people cultivate to the fullest extent their capacity for Buddhahood.

One of the Lotus Sutra's seven parables is that of the jewel in the robe: A poor man visits a friend's house, becomes drunk on wine and falls asleep. The friend has to go out on business. Concerned about the poor man, he has a priceless jewel sewn into the lining of the man's robe before departing. The poor man eventually leaves, journeying throughout the world and suffering in poverty, unaware of his friend's generous gesture. If only he could become aware of the priceless jewel inside his robe, he could alleviate much of his suffering. But he continues wandering unaware and in misery (see *The Lotus Sutra*, p. 150–51).

This story, of course, symbolizes people's unhappy wandering through life without knowing the existence of the unlimited treasure house within their lives. This is what Nichiren is talking about when he writes, "If you think the Law is outside yourself..." (WND, 3). People seek the Law everywhere but where it exists—within their own lives—so they suffer.

When we chant Nam-myoho-renge-kyo, the Law that exists within us, we should avoid succumbing to this pitfall. When we meet an obstacle, we must accept it as our challenge without blaming others for it. That way, we can savor the power of Myoho-renge-kyo and experience our own self-created happiness. With this perspective, practicing Buddhism exactly as Nichiren propagated it, we, the SGI members, have become well aware of the benefit of chanting Nam-myoho-renge-kyo.

As long as we practice faith as taught in the SGI, then none of our efforts will ever be wasted. While Nichiren admonishes that "a coward cannot have any of his prayers answered" ("The Strategy of the Lotus Sutra," WND, 1001), our lives will never become an "endless, painful austerity" because we courageously challenge ourselves to chant Nam-myoho-renge-kyo and enjoy the benefit of Buddhist practice while sharing the Mystic Law with many loved ones and friends.

In addition to becoming an "endless, painful austerity," Nichiren further explains that if we seek the Law outside ourselves, then, in spite of appearances, our Buddhist practice will be no different from the practice of a non-Buddhist teaching.

This describes exactly what is happening to Nichiren Shoshu followers. Although they enshrine the Gohonzon and chant the same Nam-myoho-renge-kyo, the essence of their faith is their dependency on priests. As long as they ask priests to pray for them at their funerals, they think that everything will turn out OK. This is nothing other than seeking the Law outside themselves, a practice that, despite its appearance, is non-Buddhist at its core.

This is exactly how it is explained in the Great Teacher T'ien-t'ai's *Great Concentration and Insight,* which Nichiren cites here as saying, "Although they study Buddhism, their views are no different from those of non-Buddhists" (WND, 4). Here, "non-Buddhists" refers to those who seem to believe in Buddhism yet maintain non-Buddhist views.

Nichiren repeatedly warns us not to seek the Law outside ourselves, and each of us must take his admonition to heart. If we run away from our obstacles and hope for some sort of external salvation, then our practice will be no different from that of a non-Buddhist. Even though Nichiren stresses the importance of practicing "fighting daimoku," from time to time people chant Nam-myoho-renge-kyo as if complaining. But if we chant while filled with complaint, then there will be no benefit. Let us always chant filled with conviction that we will definitely experience benefit, that we will definitely win. To do so is to chant the "fighting daimoku" that Nichiren taught.

NOTE:

1. *The Annotations on "Great Concentration and Insight."*

The Roots of Goodness

Whether you chant the Buddha's name,[1] recite the sutra, or merely offer flowers and incense, all your virtuous acts will implant benefits and roots of goodness in your life. With this conviction you should strive in faith. (WND, 4)

NICHIREN DAISHONIN states that every effort we make for the sake of Buddhism, no matter how insignificant it may seem, will become a source of benefit. He encourages us to have conviction in this. In terms of our practice today, the acts listed above refer to all our actions to praise and respect the Gohonzon, such as chanting Nam-myoho-renge-kyo, reciting portions of the Lotus Sutra and making offerings.

What is most important in making offerings is to do so out of sincerity. To make a sincere offering is to practice in accord with the Mystic Law; and each sincere offering is an action that will bring great benefit.

Again, as Nichiren explains, the Mystic Law exists "in your life." When you can believe this and chant Nam-myoho-renge-kyo to the Gohonzon, all your offerings will bring you infinite benefit and merit.

President Ikeda states: "Everything you do for kosen-rufu will become a source of great good fortune for you and your family. No matter how foolish people may envy or malign you, you will be praised many tenfold times by the Buddhas, bodhisattvas and heavenly deities throughout the universe, and blessed with boundless fortune and benefit, savoring 'the greatest of all joys' (*Nichiren Daishonin Gosho Zenshu*, p. 788). This is the teaching of Buddhism.

"For those who rise to the challenge at a crucial moment, all hardships will be transformed into the power to attain the life-state of Buddhahood. Nothing is wasted in Buddhism. There is no downside to faith. All of you will conclude your lives like a magnificent sunset.

"In contrast, those who persecute you—noble bodhisattvas, people as praiseworthy as the Buddha—will receive their just recompense and topple to ruin in the end. This is perfectly clear as we observe the fates of the ingrates who have abandoned their faith and betrayed their fellow members. The law of cause and effect is uncompromising" (August 20, 2004, *World Tribune*, p. 3).

NOTE

1. As used here, "the Buddha's name" denotes Nam-myoho-renge-kyo.

Ordinary Beings are the Entities of Enlightenment

The Vimalakirti Sutra states that, when one seeks the Buddhas' emancipation in the minds of ordinary beings, one finds that ordinary beings are the entities of enlightenment, and that the sufferings of birth and death are nirvana. It also states that, if the minds of living beings are impure, their land is also impure, but if their minds are pure, so is their land. There are not two lands, pure or impure in themselves. The difference lies solely in the good or evil of our minds.

It is the same with a Buddha and an ordinary being. When deluded, one is called an ordinary being, but when enlightened, one is called a Buddha. This is similar to a tarnished mirror that will shine like a jewel when polished. (WND, 4)

QUOTING FROM the Vimalakirti Sutra, Nichiren Daishonin explains that the attainment of Buddhahood depends upon one's intention. "Ordinary beings are the entities of enlightenment"—this means that the wisdom of a Buddha's enlightenment does not exist apart from the people. Although the minds of ordinary people fall sway to the influence of earthly desires, a Buddha's enlightenment appears only in the lives of ordinary people.

"The sufferings of birth and death are nirvana" means that nirvana—the truly peaceful state of a Buddha's enlightenment—will be realized in the lives of ordinary people who experience the sufferings of birth and death.

Both of these Buddhist concepts explain that Buddhas and ordinary people are not separate entities and that whether one is a Buddha or an ordinary person is solely a function of his or her mind.

Through elevating one's state of mind, the life of an ordinary person, riddled with suffering and earthly desires, can be transformed into the life of enlightenment. These concepts illustrate that an ordinary person does not need to be reborn as someone else or pass from this existence to another world in order to attain enlightenment. Instead, an ordinary person's life transformation is immediate, as expressed by the Japanese word *soku*, which translates as "are" or "are identical with."

In this regard, Nichiren states, "The single word 'identical' is symbolic of Nam-myoho-renge-kyo" (OTT, 72). In other words, through the power of Nam-myoho-renge-kyo, ordinary persons can transform their life-condition into the state of Buddhahood without having to fundamentally change who they are. Nam-myoho-renge-kyo has the power to transform at once a life of delusion into a life of enlightenment. By chanting Nam-myoho-renge-kyo, we can change all the problems we face into a source of hope and happiness.

Happiness is not the absence of hardships. Rather, we can use hardships as the springboard toward authentic happiness. Those who suffer most can become the happiest. Buddhism expounds this "mystic" transformation.

To believe that one's life and the life of a Buddha are "identical" means to chant Nam-myoho-renge-kyo with constant confidence. "Identical" corresponds to faith as expressed by the thought, *No matter what happens, I will continue practicing with sincerity.* Establishing such firm conviction is what it means to attain Buddhahood in this lifetime.

I will never lose faith in Myoho-renge-kyo. I will never retreat in faith and will always challenge myself no matter what. I will break through anything by chanting Nam-myoho-renge-kyo. When we develop such resolute faith, we will have attained Buddhahood in this lifetime.

Some, however, reject this view of Buddhahood, seeing it as a fixed point to be attained once and for all. Others insist that people cannot be described as truly having attained Buddhahood until they accomplish a goal that clearly distinguishes them from unenlightened, ordinary people.

But the life of Buddhahood is not something that appears once and forever, nor is it an image to be attained through some specific accomplishment. According to President Toda, attaining Buddhahood in this lifetime means reaching a state of absolute happiness that cannot be destroyed by anything.

In the state of Buddhahood, the unlimited power of Myoho-renge-kyo manifests in the most appropriate form at the most appropriate time. The unlimited power of the Mystic Law cannot be summed up in one particular word; it is expressed in human life as life force, wisdom, compassion, courage, endurance, good fortune, a sense of security and so on. Again, these qualities manifest when needed, enabling us to live correctly; and it is our strong faith that unleashes the infinite power of the

Mystic Law.

Buddhahood is revealed in one's life through faith, through one's mind or strong intention. For this reason, Nichiren explains, quoting from the Vimalakirti Sutra, that ordinary beings and Buddhas are not separate existences and that the impure land where ordinary beings dwell and the pure land of the Buddha are not separate places.

First, Nichiren explains the real difference between pure and impure lands. He says that when the minds of people are impure, so is their land. When the minds of people are pure, their land is also pure. State of mind is what determines the state of the land.

Next, he explains the difference between an ordinary person and a Buddha as being solely whether one is deluded or enlightened.

Nichiren refutes as being not truly Buddhist the view that the Pure Land of Perfect Bliss is located far to the west while the world we live in is the impure *saha* world.

To seek happiness elsewhere instead of where one resides is related to the point of view that separates a pure land from an impure land.

For those in the world of hell, anywhere they live, even if it is a palace, becomes a realm of hellish suffering.

For those in the world of heavenly beings, even an ordinary place becomes a palace of enjoyment.

For those in the world of Buddhahood or bodhisattvas, their land becomes the place where they fight for the realization of peace through connecting with people.

The life of a subjective being and that being's external environment are interrelated. Increasingly, people are embracing this view. Because of the oneness of life and its environment, what is most important is to elevate the life-condition of human beings.

Although there are many important issues facing today's world, the most fundamental issue is the reformation of human beings. This extremely important concept—the interconnectedness of life and its environment—is the underlying idea behind President Ikeda's efforts to promote peace, culture and education through dialogue.

President Ikeda explains: "On the spiritual level, however, I think we can say that the life-state of someone who has attained Buddhahood is what President Toda described as 'great hope.' In actuality, this great hope stems from inner confidence in one's ability to attain Buddhahood and one's grasp of the meaning of life, as well as conviction in the inherent ability of all people to become enlightened" (*The World of Nichiren Daishonin's Writings*, vol. 1, p. 130).

Polishing the Mirror

A mind now clouded by the illusions of the innate darkness of life is like a tarnished mirror, but when polished, it is sure to become like a clear mirror, reflecting the essential nature of phenomena and the true aspect of reality. Arouse deep faith, and diligently polish your mirror day and night. How should you polish it? Only by chanting Nam-myoho-renge-kyo. (WND, 4)

THROUGH THE PRACTICE of chanting Nam-myoho-renge-kyo and reciting portions of the Lotus Sutra, we can polish the mirror of our lives, which is covered by the karmic defilement of slander of the Law in previous lifetimes, and reveal the pure, vibrant life of Buddhahood inherent within us.

It is important to note that the mirror in this analogy remains the same before and after polishing. Its functionality, however, will be completely different after it is polished. Likewise, although we do not become different human beings through the practice, our lives will be purified, and how we function will be vastly different.

Through our consistent practice, we can rid our lives of the karmic impurities created through slander of the Law in our present and past lifetimes and bring forth our innate Buddhahood, which is pure and powerful.

Conclusion

If you chant Myoho-renge-kyo with deep faith in this principle, you are certain to attain Buddhahood in this lifetime. That is why the sutra states, "After I have passed into extinction, [one] should accept and uphold this sutra. Such a person assuredly and without doubt will attain the Buddha way."[1] Never doubt in the slightest. Respectfully.

Maintain your faith and attain Buddhahood in this lifetime. Nam-myoho-renge-kyo, Nam-myoho-renge-kyo. (WND, 4)

AT THE VERY END of this letter, Nichiren Daishonin emphasizes the importance of faith. Nichiren declares that with faith we can absolutely attain Buddhahood in this lifetime.

He quotes a passage from the Lotus Sutra's "Supernatural Powers of the Thus Come One" chapter, which assures us of Buddhahood as a result of our practice as Bodhisattvas of the Earth. It tells us that after the passing of Shakyamuni, those who believe in and embrace the Lotus Sutra will surely attain Buddhahood.

Once again, Nichiren admonishes us for our disbelief, saying, "Never doubt in the slightest."

President Ikeda writes: "The Bodhisattvas of the Earth are in fact Buddhas. But the term *Buddha* is inevitably taken to mean a being who is somehow transcendental or superior to ordinary human beings. The Bodhisattvas of the Earth thoroughly devote themselves to the way of bodhisattvas as people who carry out Buddhist practice. They thoroughly devote themselves to the way of human beings. This point is tremendously significant. The restoration of trust and belief in humanity will be the key to religion in the twenty-first century" (*The Wisdom of the Lotus Sutra.* vol. III, p. 272).

NOTE:

1. *The Lotus Sutra*, p. 276.

Glossary

bodhisattva   (Skt; Jpn *bosatsu*) One who aspires to enlightenment, or Buddhahood. *Bodhi* means enlightenment, and *sattva*, a living being. A person who aspires to enlightenment and carries out altruistic practice. The predominant characteristic of a bodhisattva is therefore compassion.

Bodhisattvas of the Earth (Jpn *jiyu-no-bosatsu*) An innumerable host of bodhisattvas who emerge from the earth from beneath the earth and to whom Shakyamuni Buddha entrusts the propagation of the Mystic Law, or the essence of the Lotus Sutra, in the Latter Day of the Law. They are described in the "Emerging from the Earth" (fifteenth) chapter of the Lotus Sutra. They are led by four bodhisattvas—Superior Practices, Boundless Practices, Pure Practices, Firmly Established Practices—and Superior Practices is the leader of them all. In the "Supernatural Powers" (twenty-first) chapter, Shakyamuni transfers the essence of the Lotus Sutra to the Bodhisattvas of the Earth, entrusting them with the mission of propagating it in the Latter Day of the Law.

Buddha   (Skt, Pali; Jpn *hotoke* or *butsu*) One enlightened to the eternal and ultimate truth that is the reality of all things, and who leads others to attain the same enlightenment. In Buddhism, it refers to one who has become awakened to the ultimate truth of all phenomena. The Lotus Sutra views Buddha as one who manifests the three virtues of sovereign, teacher and parent, who is enlightened to the true aspect of all phenomena, and who teaches it to people to save them from suffering. The Buddhism of Nichiren, which is based on the Lotus Sutra and regards it as Shakyamuni's most profound teaching, recognizes the potential of every person to become a Buddha.

Buddhahood The state that a Buddha has attained. The ultimate goal of Buddhist practice and the highest of the Ten Worlds. The word *enlightenment* is often used synonymously with Buddhahood. Buddhahood is regarded as a state of perfect freedom, in which one is awakened to the eternal and ultimate truth that is the reality of all things. This supreme state of life is characterized by boundless wisdom and infinite compassion. The Lotus Sutra reveals that Buddhahood is a potential in the lives of all beings.

cause and effect (1) Buddhism expounds the law of cause and effect that operates in life, ranging over past, present and future existences. This causality underlies the doctrine of karma. From this viewpoint, causes formed in the past are manifested as effects in the present. Causes formed in the present will be manifested as effects in the future. (2) From the viewpoint of Buddhist practice, cause represents the bodhisattva practice for attaining Buddhahood, and effect represents the benefit of Buddhahood. (3) From the viewpoint that, among the Ten Worlds, cause represents the nine worlds and effect represents Buddhahood, Nichiren Daishonin refers to two kinds of teachings: those that view things from the standpoint of "cause to effect" and those that approach things from the standpoint of "effect to cause." The former indicates Shakyamuni's teaching, while the latter indicates Nichiren's teaching.

daimoku (1) The title of a sutra, in particular the title of the Lotus Sutra of the Wonderful Law (Chin *Miao-fa-lien-hua-ching*; Jpn *Myoho-renge-kyo*). The title of a sutra represents the essence of the sutra. (2) The invocation of Nam-myoho-renge-kyo in Nichiren's teachings. One of his Three Great Secret Laws.

dharma A term fundamental to Buddhism that derives from a verbal root *dhri*, which means to preserve, maintain, keep or uphold. *Dharma* has a wide variety of meanings, such as law, truth, doctrine, the Buddha's teaching, decree, observance, conduct, duty, virtue, morality, religion, justice, nature, quality, character, characteristic, essence, elements of existence and phenomena. Some of the more common usages are: (1) (Often capitalized) The Law, or ultimate truth. For example, Kumarajiva translated *saddharma*, the Sanskrit word that literally means correct Law, as Wonderful Law or Mystic Law, indicating the unfathomable truth or Law that governs all phenomena. (2) The teaching of the Buddha that reveals the Law. The *Dharma* of *abhidharma* means the Buddha's doctrine, or the sutras. (3) (Often plural) Manifestations of the Law, i.e., phenomena, things, facts or existences. The word phenomena in "the true aspect of all phenomena" is the translation of *dharmas.*

earthly desires Also, illusions, defilements, impurities, earthly passions or simply desires. A generic term for all the workings of life, including desires and illusions in the general sense, that cause one's psychological and physical suffering and impede the quest for enlightenment.

five components Also, the five components of life and the five aggregates. The constituent elements of form, perception, conception, volition and consciousness that unite temporarily to form an individual living being. The five components also constitute the first of the three realms of existence.

fundamental darkness Also, fundamental ignorance. The most deeply rooted illusion inherent in life, which gives rise to all other illusions and earthly desires.

Gohonzon (Jpn) The object of devotion. The word *go* is an honorific prefix, and *honzon* means object of fundamental respect or devotion. In Nichiren Daishonin's teaching, the object of devotion has two aspects: the object of devotion in terms of the Law and the object of devotion in terms of the Person. It takes the form of a mandala inscribed on paper or on wood with characters representing the Mystic Law as well as the Ten Worlds. Nichiren Buddhism holds that all people possess the Buddha nature and can attain Buddhahood through faith in the Gohonzon.

Great Concentration and Insight One of T'ien-t'ai's three major works. This work clarifies the principle of three thousand realms in a single moment of life based on the Lotus Sutra. And it elucidates the method of meditation for observing one's mind and realizing the principle within oneself.

human revolution A concept coined by the Soka Gakkai's second president, Josei Toda, to indicate the self-reformation of an individual— the strengthening of life force and the establishment of Buddhahood —that is the goal of Buddhist practice.

kalpa An extremely long time. Sutras and treatises differ in their definitions, but *kalpas* fall into two major categories, those of measurable and immeasurable duration. There are three kinds of measurable *kalpas*; small, medium and major. One explanation sets the length of a small *kalpa* at approximately sixteen million years.

karma Potential energies residing in the inner realm of life, which manifest themselves as various results in the future. In Buddhism, karma is interpreted as meaning mental, verbal and physical action; that is, thoughts, words and deeds.

kosen-rufu Literally, to "widely declare and spread [Buddhism]," Nichiren Daishonin defines Nam-myoho-renge-kyo of the Three Great Secret Laws as the law to be widely declared and spread during the Latter Day. There are two aspects of kosen-rufu: the kosen-rufu of the entity of the Law, or the establishment of the Dai-Gohonzon, which is the basis of the Three Great Secret Laws; and the kosen-rufu of substantiation, the widespread acceptance of faith in the Dai-Gohonzon among the people.

Latter Day of the Law Also, the Latter Day. The last of the three periods following Shakyamuni Buddha's death when Buddhism falls into confusion and Shakyamuni's teachings lose the power to lead people to enlightenment. A time when the essence of the Lotus Sutra will be propagated to save all mankind.

Lotus Sutra The highest teaching of Shakyamuni Buddha, it reveals that all people can attain enlightenment and declares that his former teachings should be regarded as preparatory.

Mystic Law The ultimate Law of life and the universe. The Law of Nam-myoho-renge-kyo.

Nam-myoho-renge-kyo The ultimate Law of the true aspect of life permeating all phenomena in the universe. The invocation established by Nichiren Daishonin on April 28, 1253. Nichiren teaches that this phrase encompasses all laws and teachings within itself, and that the benefit of chanting Nam-myoho-renge-kyo includes the benefit of conducting all virtuous practices. *Nam* means "devotion to"; *myoho* means

"Mystic Law"; *renge* refers to the lotus flower, which simultaneously blooms and seeds, indicating the simultaneity of cause and effect; *kyo* means "sutra," the teaching of a Buddha.

Nichiren Daishonin The thirteenth-century Japanese Buddhist teacher and reformer who taught that all people have the potential for enlightenment. He defined the universal Law as Nam-myoho-renge-kyo and established the Gohonzon as the object of devotion for all people to attain Buddhahood.

saha world This world, which is full of sufferings. In the Chinese version of Buddhist scriptures, the Sanskrit *saha* is translated as "endurance." The term *saha* world suggests that the people who live in this world must endure sufferings. It is also identified as an impure land, in contrast to a pure land. The *saha* world is the land where Shakyamuni Buddha makes his appearance and, enduring various hardships, instructs living beings. Some Buddhist scriptures, including the Lotus Sutra, hold that the *saha* world can be transformed in the Land of Eternally Tranquil Light, or that the *saha* world is in itself the Land of Eternally Tranquil Light.

secret and mystic expedient The secret and mystic expedient is the heart of the "Expedient Means" chapter of the Lotus Sutra. *Secret* of "secret and mystic expedient" refers to the fact that it is only known and understood by Buddhas. In other words, only Buddhas know the truth that all living beings are Buddhas. Though the truth is hidden, under certain external conditions it can be revealed. That unfathomable reality of life is called "mystic." In terms of the Ten Worlds, the world of Buddhahood is hidden in the lives of the people of the nine worlds. Upon contact with the appropriate external conditions, however, it can be manifested within the nine worlds. This wonder is called mystic. We ordinary people are Buddhas, just as we are. This is inconceivable, beyond the scope of our comprehension. Therefore, it is "mystic." Those who don't believe in the Lotus Sutra cannot understand this. Therefore, it is "secret." The doctrine of the secret and mystic expedient teaches us that even people who do not yet uphold the Mystic Law, though it is likely they don't know it themselves (for it is secret), are actually one with the Mystic Law (hence, 'mystic'). Because of this, in the depths of their being, they are seeking the Mystic Law.

Shakyamuni   Also, Siddhartha Gautama. Born in India (present-day southern Nepal) about three thousand years ago, he is the first recorded Buddha and founder of Buddhism. For fifty years, he expounded various sutras (teachings), culminating in the Lotus Sutra.

Soka Gakkai International   A worldwide Buddhist association that promotes peace and individual happiness based on the teachings of the Nichiren school of Buddhism, with more than twelve million members in more than 190 countries and territories. Its headquarters is in Tokyo, Japan.

sufferings of birth and death are nirvana   The Lotus Sutra teaches that, by awakening to one's innate Buddha nature, one can reach the state of nirvana in his or her present form as an ordinary person who possesses earthly desires and undergoes the sufferings of birth and death. It reveals the principle that the sufferings of birth and death are none other than nirvana. From the standpoint of the Lotus Sutra, birth and death are two integral phases of eternal life. Nirvana, therefore, is not the cessation of birth and death, but a state of enlightenment experienced as one repeats the cycle of birth and death. The sufferings of birth and death are nirvana, or enlightenment, are inseparable: it is not necessary to extinguish one in order to attain the other.

Ten Worlds   Ten life-conditions that a single entity of life manifests. Originally the Ten Worlds were viewed as distinct physical places, each with its own particular inhabitants. In light of the Lotus Sutra, they are interpreted as potential conditions of life inherent in each individual. The ten are: (1) hell, (2) hunger, (3) animality, (4) anger, (5) humanity or tranquility, (6) rapture, (7) learning, (8) realization, (9) bodhisattva and (10) Buddhahood.

three thousand realms in a single moment of life (Jpn *ichinen sanzen*)   A philosophical system established by T'ien-t'ai. The "three thousand realms" indicates the varying aspects and phases that life assumes at each moment. At each moment, life manifests one of the Ten Worlds.

Each of these worlds possesses the potential for all ten within itself, thus making one hundred possible worlds. Each of these hundred worlds possesses the ten factors and operates within each of the three realms of existence, thus making three thousand realms.

T'ien-t'ai (538–597) Referred to also as Chih-i, T'ien-t'ai Chih-che, the Great Teacher T'ien-t'ai and the Great Teacher Chih-che. The founder of the T'ien-t'ai school in China. After studying at Mount Ta-su under Nan-yueh, he became known for his profound lectures on the Lotus Sutra. He refuted the scriptural classifications formulated by the ten major Buddhist schools of his day, and classified all of Shakyamuni's sutras into five periods and eight teachings, demonstrating the supremacy of the Lotus Sutra.

Josei Toda The second president of the Soka Gakkai. Inaugurated on May 3, 1951, President Toda rebuilt the Soka Gakkai after World War II, surpassing his membership goal of 750,000 families.

Toki Jonin A lay follower of Nichiren Daishonin who lived in Wakamiya, Katsushika District of Shimosa Province, Japan. Toki became Nichiren's follower around 1254, the year after Nichiren first declared his teaching at Seicho-ji. He was a man of considerable erudition, and Nichiren entrusted him with a number of his more important works including "The Object of Devotion for Observing the Mind," one of his five major writings. When Nichiren was in exile on Sado from 1271 through 1274, Toki Jonin, with Shijo Kingo, served as a rallying point for his followers. Toki Jonin also received the "Letter from Sado."

true aspect of all phenomena The ultimate truth or reality that permeates all phenomena and is in no way separate from them. The "Expedient Means" chapter of the Lotus Sutra defines this as the ten factors of life, and Nichiren Daishonin defined it as Nam-myoho-renge-kyo.

Vimalakirti Sutra A Mahayana sutra about the wealthy layman Vimalakirti in Vaishali, translated into Chinese in 406 by Kumarajiva. The full title of Kumarajiva's version is the Sutra on the Expositions of Vimalakirti. The Sanskirt original is not extant. The sutra sets forth the ideal of the Mahayana bodhisattva, which is to draw no distinction between self and others.